Date: 2/8/12

**J 636.8 STE
Stevens, Kathryn,
Cats /**

PET CARE FOR KIDS

CATS

BY KATHRYN STEVENS

Published by The Child's World®
1980 Lookout Drive • Mankato, MN 56003-1705
800-599-READ • www.childsworld.com

Acknowledgments
The Child's World®: Mary Berendes, Publishing Director
The Design Lab: Kathleen Petelinsek, Design and Page Production

Photo Credits: Dreamstime/Drazen Vukelic: 5; iStockphoto.com/
Alexey Stiop: front cover, 1, 3, 16, 20 (toys); iStockphoto.com/
Amanda Rohde: 11; iStockphoto.com/Angelika Schwarz: 8 (cat);
iStockphoto.com/Ebru Baraz: 13; iStockphoto.com/Ethan Myerson: front cover, 1, 3, 6, 20 (kibble); iStockphoto.com/Feng Yu: 12;
iStockphoto.com/Ina Peters: front cover, 3 (jumping); iStockphoto.com/James Steidl: 14; iStockphoto.com/Julia Pivovarova: 19; iStockphoto.com/Kamil Karpiel: 8, 20 (brush); iStockphoto.com/Katherine Welles: 15; iStockphoto.com/Nina Shannon: 10; iStockphoto.com/orix3: front cover, back cover, 1, 3, 16, 20 (ball); iStockphoto.com/Sharon Dominick: 7; iStockphoto.com/Sondra Paulson: front cover, back cover, 1, 3, 6 (catnip); iStockphoto.com/Tony Campbell: front cover (batting); iStockphoto.com/Willie B. Thomas: 9; iStockphoto.com/Yulia Podlesnova: 17; PhotoDisc: front cover, back cover, 1, 3, 4 (various), 18, 21, 22, 24

Library of Congress Cataloging-in-Publication Data
Stevens, Kathryn, 1954–
    Cats / by Kathryn Stevens.
        p. cm. — (Pet care for kids)
    Includes index.
    ISBN 978-1-60253-180-2 (library bound)
    1. Cats—Juvenile literature. I. Title. II. Series.
    SF445.7.S75 2009
    636.8—dc22   2008039999

Printed in the United States of America
Mankato, Minnesota
January, 2010
PA02043

NOTE TO PARENTS AND EDUCATORS

The Pet Care for Kids series is written for children who want to be part of the pet experience but are too young to be in charge of pets themselves. These books are intended to provide a kid-friendly supplement to more detailed information adults need to know about choosing and caring for different types of pets. They can help youngsters learn how to live happily with the animals in their lives, and, with adults' help and supervision, grow into responsible animal caretakers later on.

CONTENTS

CATS AS PETS

There are lots of cats in need of good homes. And cats can make wonderful pets! But getting a cat is a big decision. Cats can live for a long time. They live for 15 years or even 20. They need people who will care for them the whole time.

▸ This cat is 16 years old. She has lived with the same family her whole life.

◂ This kitten is only a few weeks old. She needs people who will care for her for many years.

GOOD FOOD

Cats need good food that keeps them healthy and strong. Crunchy dried cat food is good for cats' teeth. Cats love juicy, smelly canned food, too! Cats also need clean water to drink.

▶ These cats are enjoying some smelly, fishy cat food. Cats love the smell and taste of fish!

◀ Crunchy dried food keeps cats' teeth clean.

GOOD HEALTH

Cats need visits to an animal doctor, or **vet**. The vet makes sure the cat is healthy. The vet also gives shots to keep the cat from getting sick. Cats like to keep themselves clean. They lick their fur to clean it. Long-haired cats need **grooming**.

▶ A vet is looking at this kitten's ears.

◀ This cat is cleaning her paw.

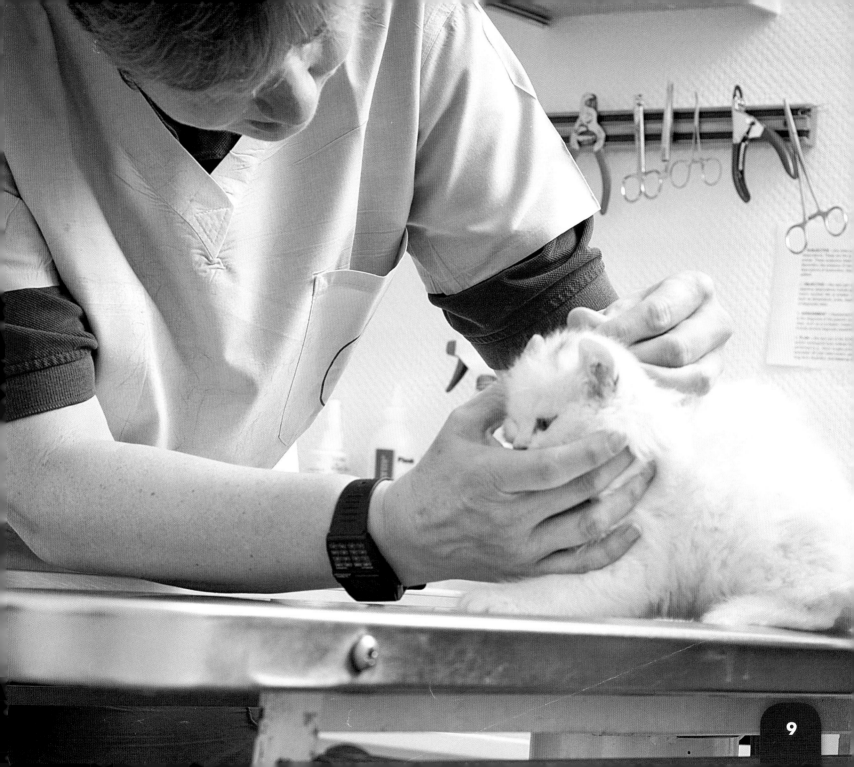

Cats have sharp claws. They like to scratch on things. A scratching post keeps them from scratching the furniture. Indoor cats also need a place to go to the bathroom. They use a box filled with **litter**. The litter box should be cleaned every day.

▶ This scratching post is also a great hiding place.

▼ This cat has a nice, clean litter box.

SAFETY

Cats that live outside face many dangers. They can get hurt or sick. Indoor cats live longer, safer lives. But they need to be kept safe, too. They need to be handled gently. They must be kept from things that could hurt them.

▶ This kitten loves playing with yarn. But eating it could harm her.

◀ Eating rubber bands can make cats very sick.

Cats are very **curious**. They love to **explore**. But exploring can get them into trouble. Sometimes they crawl into small places. Sometimes they climb too high. Then they can get stuck!

▶ This cat climbed way up in a tree. Now he cannot get down.

◀ Cats love to crawl into paper bags.

PLAYTIME

Kittens love to play. Many adult cats like to play, too. Cats like to pretend they are hunting. They sneak up on toys. They chase the toys and jump on them. They bat the toys with their paws. These things all remind the cats of hunting.

▸ This cat is sneaking up on something.

▾ There are lots of fun toys for cats.

LOTS OF LOVE!

Some cats like to be cuddled. They love to curl up on people's laps. Other cats are not so cuddly. But they still might like to be petted. Listen for their purring sound. A cat's purring lets you know it is happy!

This girl and her cat are good friends.

This cat is happy— and sleepy!

18

NEEDS:

* good food
* clean water
* a litter box
* a nice place to sleep
* toys
* grooming
* visits to the vet

DANGERS:

* running loose
* some kinds of houseplants
* household poisons
* getting stuck
* dogs that chase cats
* rubber bands, ribbons, or
  strings they can swallow

EARS:
Cats have very good hearing.

EYES:
Cats see well in the dark.

COAT:
Cats come in many colors. Their fur often has pretty patterns.

WHISKERS:
Cats' whiskers can feel the slightest touch.

CLAWS:
Cats have very sharp claws. They keep them hidden when they are not using them.

TAIL:
When cats are upset, their tail twitches.

GLOSSARY

curious *(KYUR-ee-us)* Curious means interested in things.

explore *(ek-SPLOR)* To explore is to go to new places or try new things.

grooming *(GROO-ming)* Grooming an animal is cleaning and brushing it.

litter *(LIH-tur)* Cat litter is made for places where cats go to the bathroom.

vet *(VET)* A vet is a doctor who takes care of animals. Vet is short for "veterinarian" *(vet-rih-NAYR-ee-un)*.

TO FIND OUT MORE

Books:

Miller, Michaela. *Cats*. Des Plaines, IL: Heinemann Interactive Library, 1998.

Roca, Núria, and Rosa M. Curto. *Our New Cat*. Hauppauge, NY: Barron's Educational Series, 2006.

Royston, Angela. *Kitten*. New York: DK Publishing, 2007.

Video/DVD:

Paws, Claws, Feathers & Fins: A Kid's Guide to Happy, Healthy Pets. Goldhil Learning Series (Video 1993, DVD 2005).

Web Sites:

Visit our Web page for lots of links about pet care:
http://www.childsworld.com/links

Note to parents, teachers, and librarians: We routinely verify our Web links to make sure they are safe, active sites—so encourage your readers to check them out!

INDEX

ABOUT THE AUTHOR
Kathryn Stevens has authored and edited many books for young readers, including books on animals ranging from grizzly bears to fleas. She's a lifelong pet-lover and currently cares for a big, huggable pet-therapy dog named Fudge.

INDEX